audio access included

slow blues
HARMONICA

lessons, licks & backing tracks

BY STEVE COHEN

PLAYBACK+
Speed • Pitch • Balance • Loop

To access audio visit:
www.halleonard.com/mylibrary

Enter Code
5385-8763-7507-0710

Steve Cohen can be found through his website
www.stevecohenblues.com

ISBN 978-1-5400-4678-9

Visit Hal Leonard Online at
www.halleonard.com

Contact us:
Hal Leonard
7777 West Bluemound Road
Milwaukee, WI 53213
Email: info@halleonard.com

In Europe, contact:
Hal Leonard Europe Limited
42 Wigmore Street
Marylebone, London, W1U 2RN
Email: info@halleonardeurope.com

In Australia, contact:
Hal Leonard Australia Pty. Ltd.
4 Lentara Court
Cheltenham, Victoria, 3192 Australia
Email: info@halleonard.com.au

introduction

This book is intended for intermediate to advanced diatonic harmonica players. The examples are comprised of solos that were improvised over 16 different songs with the idea of playing over a variety of slow blues changes and feels. There are many blues harmonica techniques used here, including:

- Bent notes (there are seven bends on the low end, six on the high end)
- Warbles (sometimes called "shakes" or "trills")
- Bent warbles
- Chords and octaves
- Bent chords
- Vibrato (several different kinds) and hand wah
- Overblowing in the middle register
- Glissandos and octave glissandos
- Riffs and licks
- Four different keys and crosses
- Liberal use of all three registers of the instrument

These 16 tunes are segregated to some degree by the techniques used in each tune. Generally, the easier examples are first, with harder techniques and combined techniques coming later. For instance, the first tune has no bends at all. The first four examples have no warbles or chords. High-note work is mostly concentrated into tunes 7 and 8. Minor-pitched tunes using 2nd, 3rd, and 4th position are introduced in numbers 9 through 12. There are no overblows until numbers 14 and 15. There are no octave glissandos until the last example, etc. There is more detailed information on how to achieve these techniques in the previous four books I have written, all published by Hal Leonard.

Regarding the songs themselves, I've written and recorded these tunes using a variety of blues changes and variations, including 8- and 12-bar progressions, minor-key examples, jazzy feels, and country blues feels. Each tune has two complete progressions: the first chorus segues to the second, as any blues song might, and the second chorus resolves to the song's ending. Each of the 16 tunes also has two audio tracks: a demo track with full band and a play-along track.

My harmonica part has been transcribed note for note in standard notation and harmonica tab. Each piece is preceded by a brief summary defining what kind of blues progression and/or feel the song contains, typifying what playing techniques are employed, as well as what key the song is in, and which cross I've used. Regardless of the key of the song, a single-row, 10-hole diatonic harmonica pitched in the key of C is used on all examples.

All the harmonica work was recorded using a clean vocal mic tone. The nuances of the playing can be best heard without a distorted, hand-held, cupped mic sound, although that kind of approach would also be appropriate for many of these songs.

#1 BASICS

12-bar – Key of G – 2nd position

This tune is a basic 12-bar blues progression with no variations. It's a shuffle in 4/4 time. There's no quick change (IV chord in the second bar) and no movement to the V chord at the end of the first chorus.

The playing is basic—no bends, chords, warbles, glissandos, or other effects. All the notes are played as they naturally occur on the harmonica. The second chorus starts with a descending, four-note, three-interval lick, which is echoed in the upper register in the seventh and eighth bars. The turnaround repeated in both progressions is a well-known lick.

 AUDIO TRACK
1 DEMO
2 PLAY-ALONG

Chorus 1

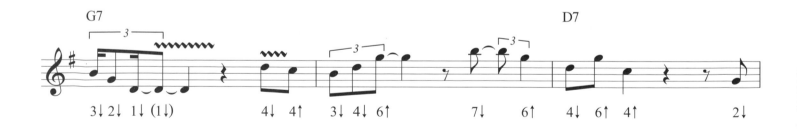

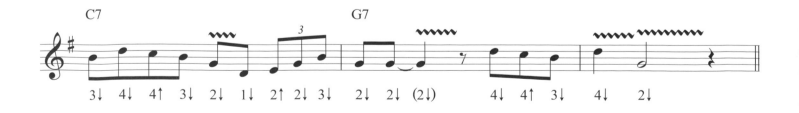

contents

Chorus 2

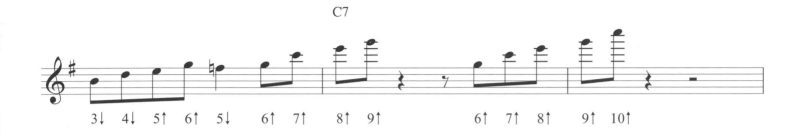

#2 B.B.

12-bar – Key of G – 2nd position

Three tempo clicks precede three pickup notes to start this 12-bar blues written in 12/8 time. The progression is typical, with a couple standard variations including a quick change (IV chord in the second bar) and movement to the V chord in the 12th bar of the first chorus.

The playing includes some easy bends on the low end to accommodate the basic chord changes. Notice the curved lines directly behind the first two notes on the staff in the second measure. These are fall-offs: hold the notes and bend them down at the tail end. How far you bend is up to you. Most of the vibratos in the tune are the common-variety throat vibratos, however, there are two ruffle vibratos in bar 8. Use your uvula or soft palate for these, which gives a raspy sound.

Rhythmically speaking, 12/8 time is made up of 12 beats per measure—three beats in each of the four pulses (or strong beats). You'll notice several four-note-per-pulse groupings in the second chorus (look for the bracketed "4" shown above the note staff for each group). Playing four evenly divided notes in the space usually occupied by three is an effective way to add rhythmic interest to your playing. Also worth mentioning: rests can be substituted for notes in these quadruplets.

◑ AUDIO TRACK
3 DEMO
4 PLAY-ALONG

*Ruffle vibrato

Chorus 2

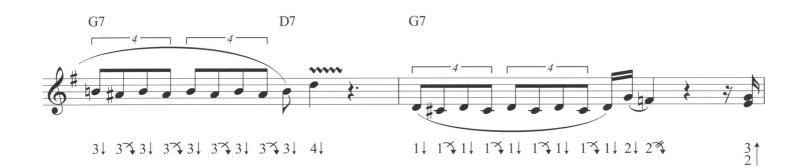

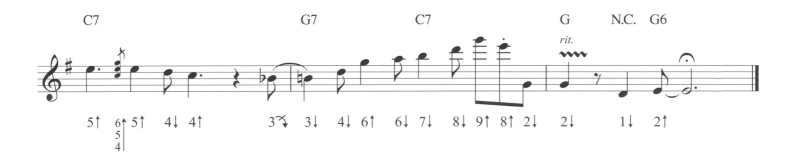

#3 KEY

8-bar – Key of G – 2nd position

This blues progression is in the family of 8-bar blues songs that move to the V chord in the second bar, like "Key to the Highway" and "Trouble in Mind."

This example is a shuffle, and triplets are featured prominently in the harp part (notice the many uses of "3" above the note staff). Normally in 4/4 time, beats consist of two eighth notes of even duration. But in a shuffle, the first of the two eighths is held longer than normal and the second is shorter than normal—actually the first is twice as long as the second. That's why triplets fit so easily in a shuffle.

The solo includes bends on the low end. It also features an ascending lick for the turnaround in the first chorus, while the second chorus ends with a classic turnaround lick in the middle register.

AUDIO TRACK
5 DEMO
6 PLAY-ALONG

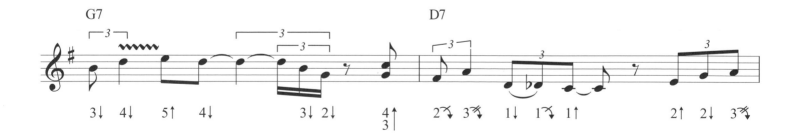

Chorus 2

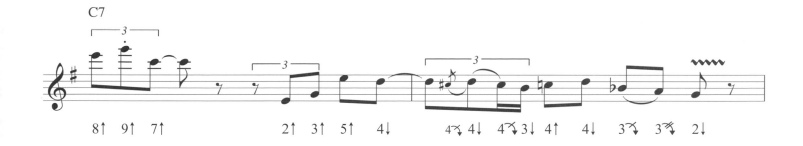

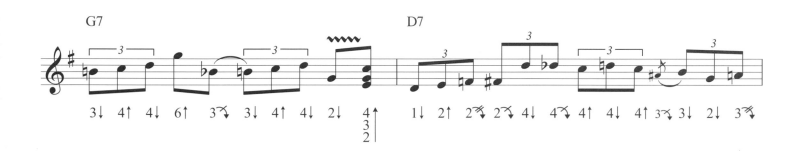

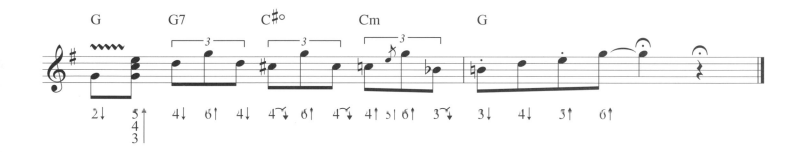

#4 POOR MAN

8-bar – Key of G – 2nd position

Like the previous tune, this is in the family of 8-bar blues. What sets this one apart is the inclusion of the I–VI–II–V chord progression; but unlike the version common in jazz, here all four chords are major. This track opens with a four-bar intro: the I–VI–II–V followed by a turnaround. The choruses include blue notes sparingly, so the tune has a "happy" vibe. Note that it goes to a minor IV chord in bar 4 of both choruses.

A rhythmic trick is featured in the first two bars of the second chorus. Visually, they're harder to spot than the bracketed groupings in previous tunes. Here, look for the groups of four sixteenth notes per beat. This tune is a shuffle, so squeezing four equally spaced notes in the same space as a three-note triplet is an effective way to shake things up a bit.

The playing involves incremental descending bends in the first bar of the intro and in the turnaround toward the end of the song. The latter features draw bends on hole 3: natural, down a half step, down a whole step, and down a step and a half. Use your tongue to separate each note rather than slurring them together.

🔊 **AUDIO TRACK**
7 DEMO
8 PLAY-ALONG

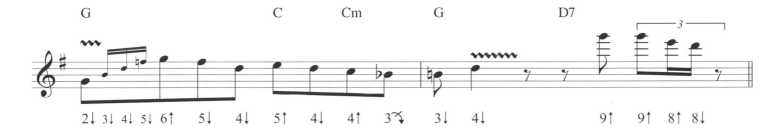

Chorus 2

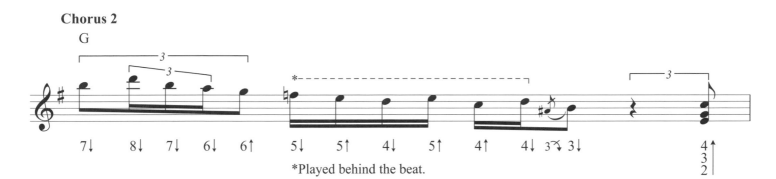

*Played behind the beat.

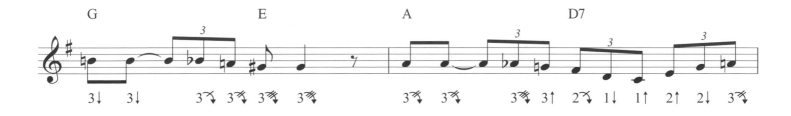

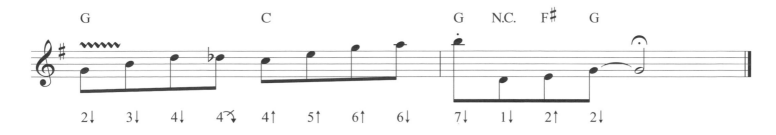

#5 BIZ

8-bar – Key of G – 2nd position

Here's an 8-bar slow blues that employs a III (B7) to IV (C7) chord transition in the second and third bars respectively, followed by ascending inversions of a C# diminished 7th chord.

Like "B.B.," this one's written in 12/8 time. Not to get too technical, but 12/8 and 4/4 are quite similar. When you compare a measure filled with eighth-note triplets in 4/4 time (four beats per measure with three evenly spaced notes per beat, for a total of 12 evenly spaced notes) with a full measure of eighth notes in 12/8 (12 evenly spaced eighth notes), they sound identical. In general, writing in 12/8 eliminates a bunch of notational clutter, but there are instances where writing in 12/8 can obscure basic rhythms. One such location is the third measure of the second chorus. For ease of reading, imagine this bar in 4/4 time played as four evenly spaced eighth notes in the first half of the measure (count: 1 & 2 &), followed by an eighth note, eighth rest, eighth note, eighth rest (count: 3 & 4 &) to complete the measure.

The playing includes bent notes to accommodate the chord changes. There is also a series of five low-end warbles (trills) bridging the two choruses, the last of which features a bent warble. There is also a series of three paired 32nd-note glisses in the second chorus (bars 5 and 6).

🔊 **AUDIO TRACK**
9 DEMO
10 PLAY-ALONG

*Played behind the beat.

14

Chorus 2

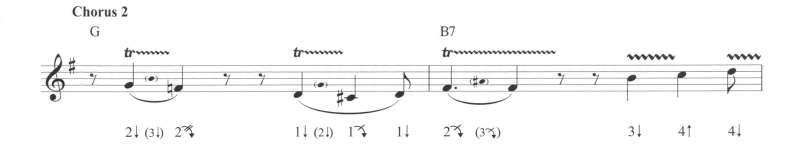

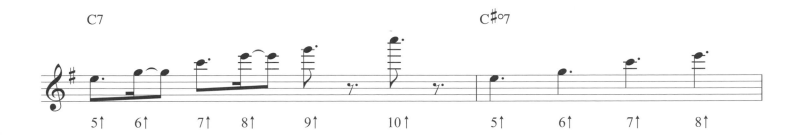

*Played behind the beat.

(This page left blank to facilitate page turns.)

#6 MUD

12-bar – Key of G – 2nd position

This example is in the style of a slow country blues tune. The progression starts with the turnaround. The first chorus bounces to the IV chord (quick change) in the second bar and to the V chord in the third and eighth bars.

Grace notes: we've seen a few here and there in the preceding solos, but there are many more in this tune.
Grace notes are the tiny notes on the staff (and their corresponding small tab numbers). They're played quickly and are often used for the starting notes of bends. They are also used for ornamentations, such as multi-note glissandos—two of which are in bar 7 of the first chorus. Play these glisses as rapidly as you can. Grace notes are transitional notes (they take you from here to there) and technically don't have rhythmic time values on their own—they always rob time from the adjacent full-size notes.

The playing involves lots of hand wah—a type of vibrato. At times, the phrasing follows the guitar in a call-and-response pattern. There are warbles and bent warbles in the first chorus and some pronounced vibratos throughout.

AUDIO TRACK
11 DEMO
12 PLAY-ALONG

17

Chorus 1

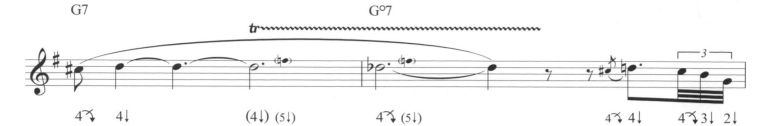

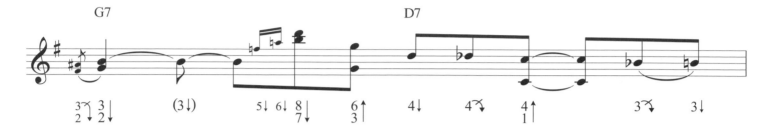

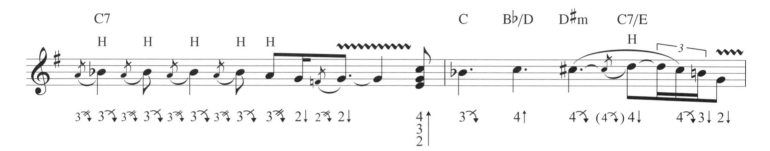

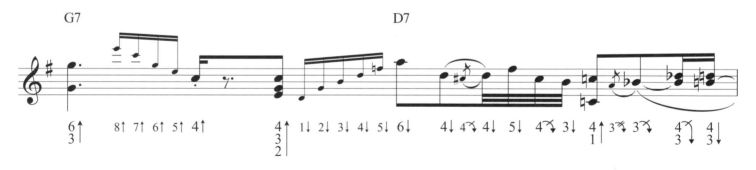

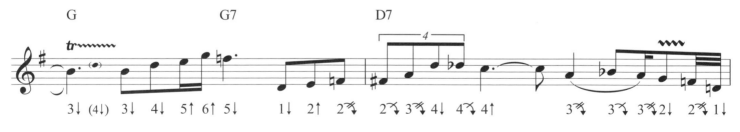

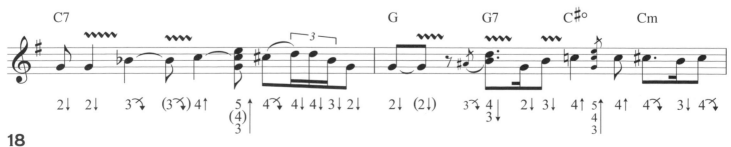

Chorus 2

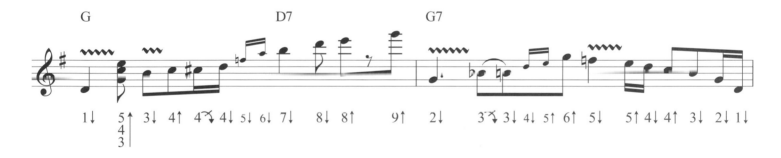

#7 HOOCH

12-bar – Key of C – 1st position

This tune is in 4/4 with a stop-time format. To help get the tune up and running, we've included rhythm slashes above the note staff for the first couple of bars to represent the phrasing of the guitar and bass. This stop-time 12-bar chord progression omits the usual movement to the IV chord in the fifth and sixth bars, but still follows the 12-bar pattern of moving to the V chord in the ninth bar and IV chord in the tenth bar.

The playing features some slow low-end warbles, hand wahs, and bent notes that purposefully do not sound 100% in tune in the first chorus. The second chorus involves extensive high-note blow bends. It also contains the turnaround found in example 3, "Key," except it's played in the high register with high-note bends. There are also some bent high-note triplets and high-note licks.

🔊 **AUDIO TRACK**
13 DEMO
14 PLAY-ALONG

20

#8 FEELING

12-bar – Key of C – 1st position

This song is a regulation 12-bar with no quick change.

The playing starts with high-note work in the first chorus, including warbles, bent warbles, high-note bends, and high-note warble bends. The second chorus contains low-end, 1st-position warbles and some unconventional low-end warble bends. Sometimes both the primary note and the trilled note are bent, and sometimes only one or the other are bent. The tune ends with an octave/chord warble: tongue block the octave as usual, but trill by quickly and continually removing and adding your tongue on holes 2 and 3.

🔊 **AUDIO TRACK**
15 DEMO
16 PLAY-ALONG

Chorus 2

23

#9 MAGIC

12-bar – Key of G minor – 2nd position

This tune is a standard 12-bar progression in 12/8 time in the key of G minor.

The playing in the first progression mixes two familiar guitar licks: one borrowed from Magic Sam and another from Big Bill Broonzy. The opening riff features staccatoed notes. The term *staccato* means to play a note for a shorter duration than normal. It's indicated by a dot above or below the notehead in standard notation. Use the tip of your tongue to regulate air flow. Octaves and three- and four-note chords appear interchangeably in bars 4 and 6 of the first chorus. The second chorus has octave warbles and glisses (this time written full size and in rhythm) in bars 1, 2, and 3, and employs high-note bends in bars 4 and 5 before returning to the original lick.

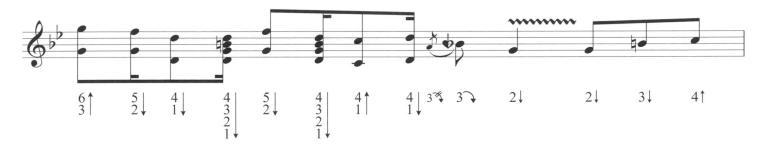

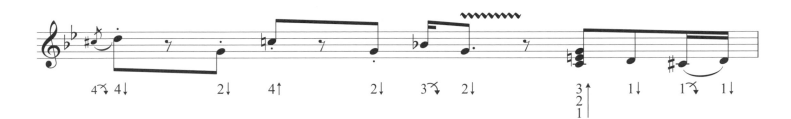

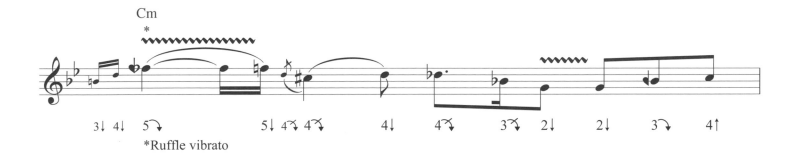

*Ruffle vibrato

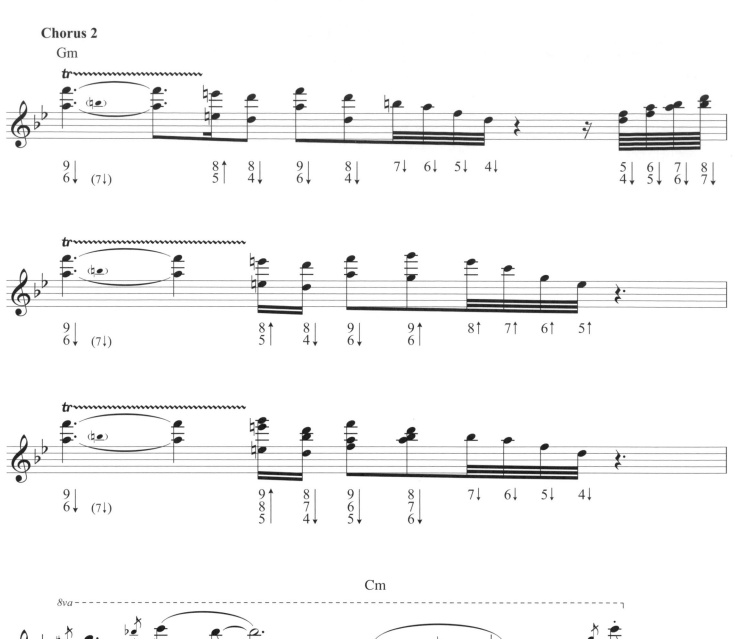

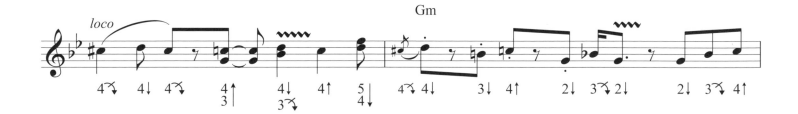

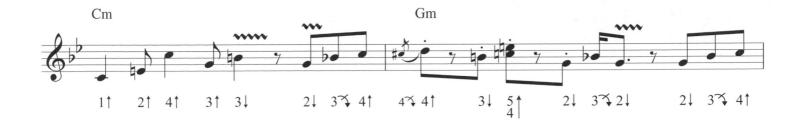

#10 BURYING

12-bar – Key of D minor – 3rd position

This song is in D minor and is a standard 12-bar progression with no quick change.

The playing features strong vibrato, long, gradual incremental bends, and warble bends. There are also octaves, octave warbles, one ruffle vibrato note, and one glissando in the second chorus.

🔊 AUDIO TRACK
19 DEMO
20 PLAY-ALONG

28

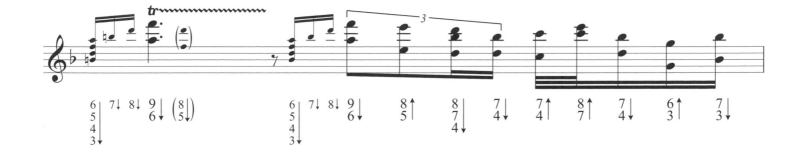

**Ruffle vibrato
*Played as even eighth notes.

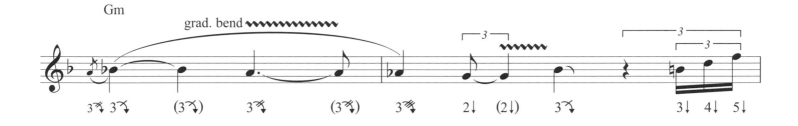

***Played as even eighth notes.

#11 HELP

12-bar – Key of G minor – 2nd position

This song is in G minor and has the fastest tempo so far. It is a standard 12-bar progression without a quick change.

The playing includes hand wah, bends, and some percussive accents-notice the pointed "hats" over the notes in measures 6 and 7 (their true name is *marcato*). Give these notes emphasis with strong air flow. You'll also see that each marcato contains a staccato dot, so play them short. These accents have a distinctive bark when playing chords, which adds contrast to the single-note lines. You'll also find chords interspersed in the second chorus; they allow the rapid release of air to facilitate phrases that extend for several measures between pauses.

AUDIO TRACK
21 DEMO
22 PLAY-ALONG

Chorus 2

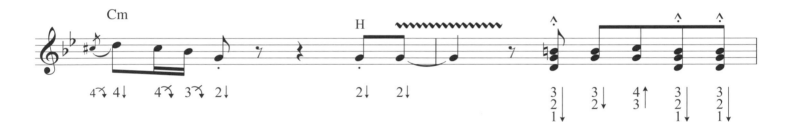

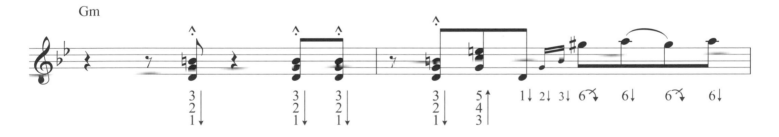

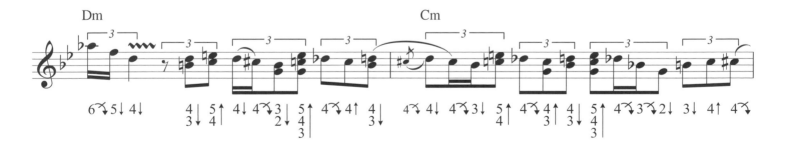

#12 THRILL

12-bar – Key of A minor – 4th position

This tune is in A minor. It has a funk feel and is a 12-bar with the variation of a #V chord in the ninth bar. Notice that it's the only 4/4 tune so far that's not a shuffle.

The playing is in 4th position, where most notes fall easily into a nice-sounding minor scale. There is a four-note descending line in the second progression, a lick that I occasionally use to employ scales in soloing. After playing four descending notes from the minor scale, move up one hole and start the pattern over again. If the fourth note was a blow, then start the next phrase with a blow. If it was a draw, start with a draw. This holds true for most of the lick. There are also a couple of triplets in the first chorus and a ruffle vibrato that morphs into a warble in the second chorus.

🔊 AUDIO TRACK
23 DEMO
24 PLAY-ALONG

Chorus 1

♩ = 90

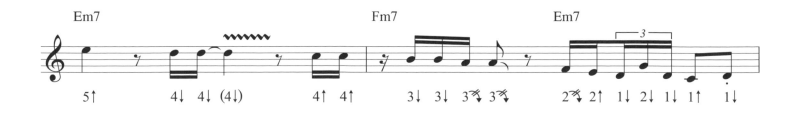

Chorus 2

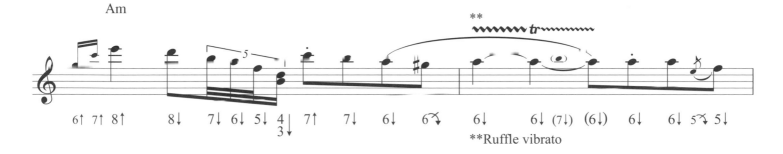

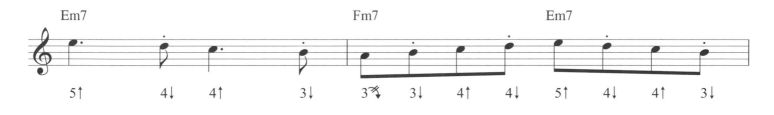

#13 HAD FUN

12-bar – Key of G – 2nd position

This is a standard 12-bar progression with no quick change.

The playing in the first chorus involves some bent chords and a great repeating lick (triplets within triplets).
In measures 10 and 11, there's a two-note, descending-3rds, A minor scale lick played over the IV and I chords.
The second chorus is made up of a four-note repeating lick followed by a bend. The first portion is played in a straight, 32nd-note rhythm, so there are eight notes—twice through the four-note pattern—per beat. Variations add interest and accommodate the chord changes.

AUDIO TRACK
25 DEMO
26 PLAY-ALONG

Chorus 1

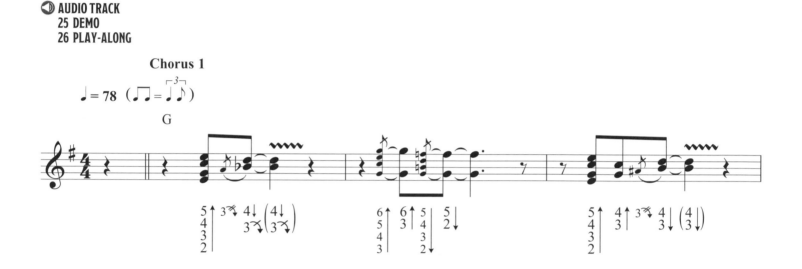

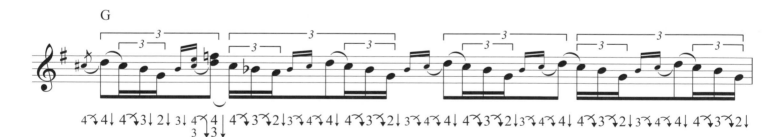

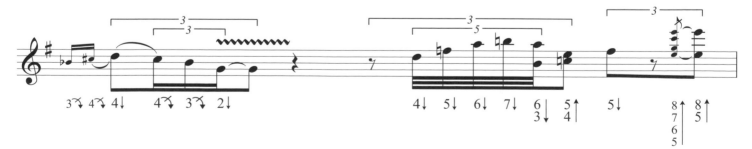

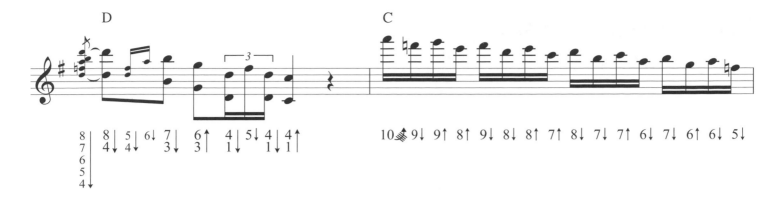

Chorus 2

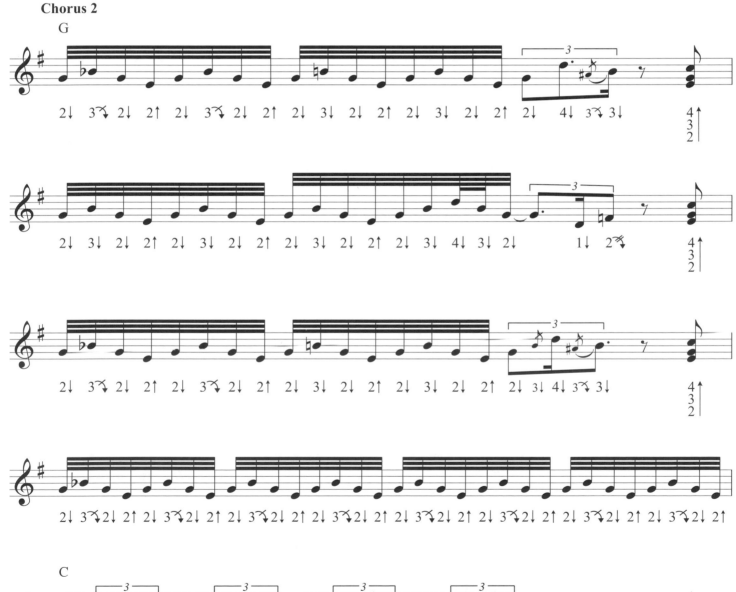

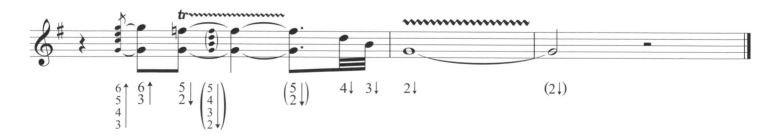

(This page left blank to facilitate page turns.)

#14 WAY I FEEL

12-bar – Key of G – 2nd position

This song is a standard 12-bar progression with a jazzy feel that uses chromatic background chords to lead into the I, IV, and V chords.

The playing includes seven overblown notes for a more chromatic approach. At the end of the first chorus, there's a lick made up of three ascending notes paired into a sextuplet (six evenly spaced notes in a beat). After two beats, the pattern starts over again but on a lower note. Drop down once more to begin the second chorus.

AUDIO TRACK
27 DEMO
28 PLAY-ALONG

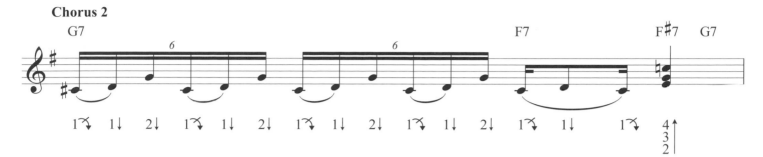

Chorus 2

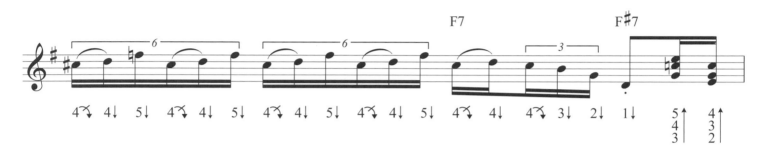

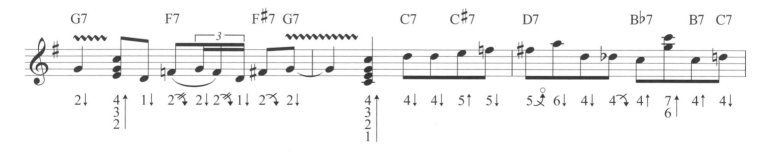

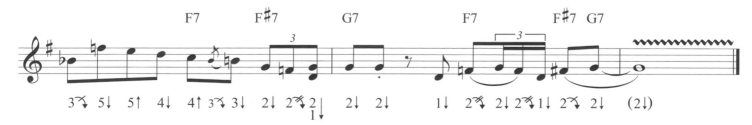

#15 PARKER'S

12-bar – Key of G – 2nd position

This tune is a 12-bar slow blues progression with a few different substitute chord changes, including a quick change, a diminished chord, descending chromatic chords, and a II–V chord change leading to a chromatic turnaround. It's uptown jazzy blues.

The playing involves overblowing on three notes, chord and octave playing, and incremental bending.

 AUDIO TRACK
29 DEMO
30 PLAY-ALONG

Chorus 1

*Circles above bend arrows denote overblown notes.

40

Chorus 2

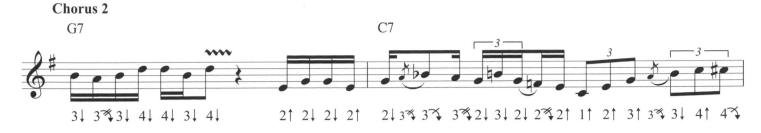

*Played as even eighth notes.

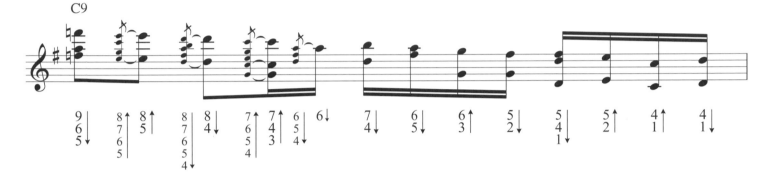

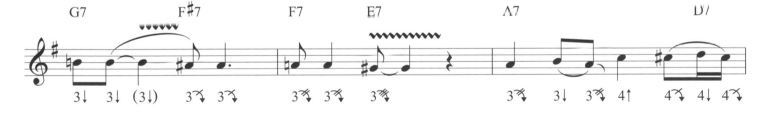

Freely

#16 DRIVING WHEEL

12-bar – Key of G – 2nd position

This song is a standard 12-bar with no quick change.

The playing in both choruses emphasizes octave and chord playing, as well as bent warbles. On first listen, you may not notice the grace-note chords that precede the octaves in the opening lick. They're subtle but add dimension to the octaves. Now that you know they're there, you'll find them throughout the tune. The second chorus features octave and single-note glissandos, and a whole lot more.

🔊 AUDIO TRACK
31 DEMO
32 PLAY-ALONG

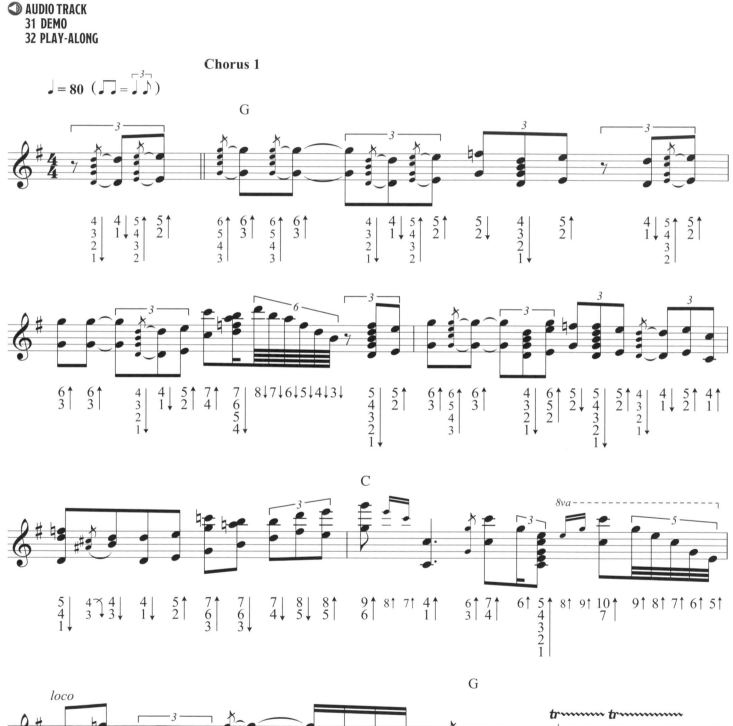

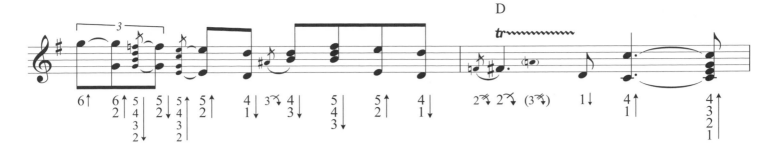

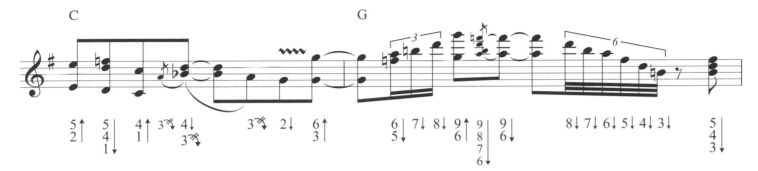

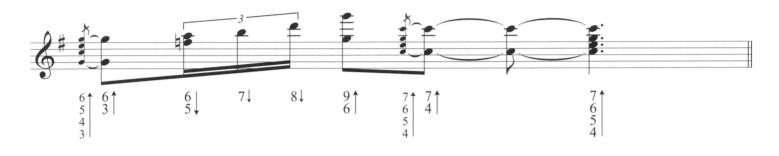

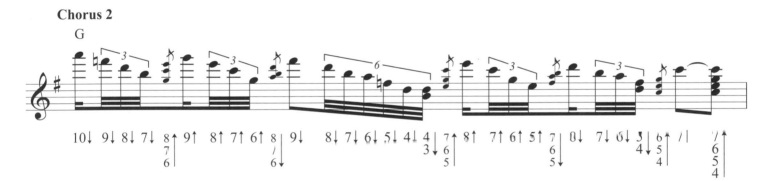

Chorus 2

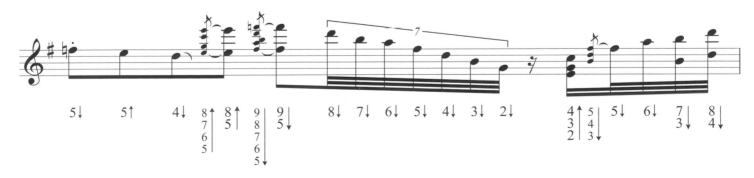

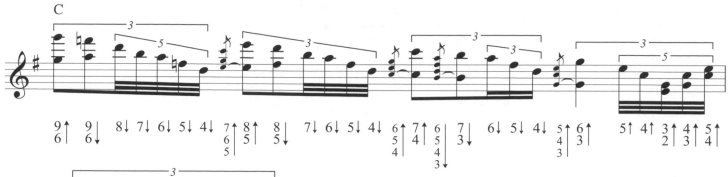

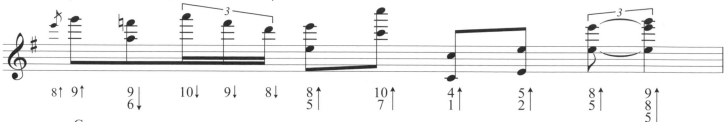

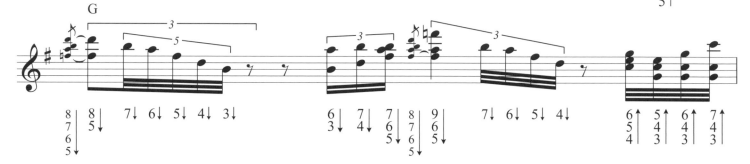

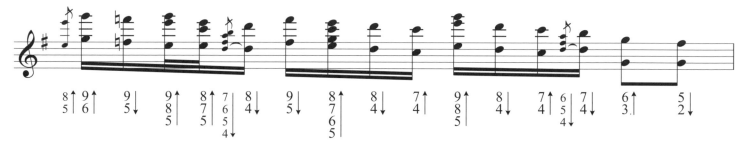

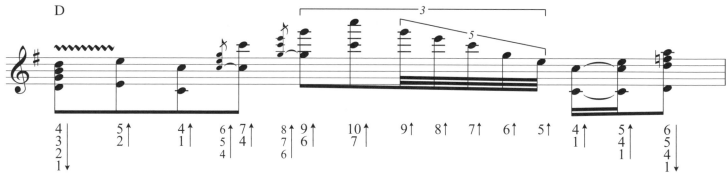

C HARP NOTE RECAP

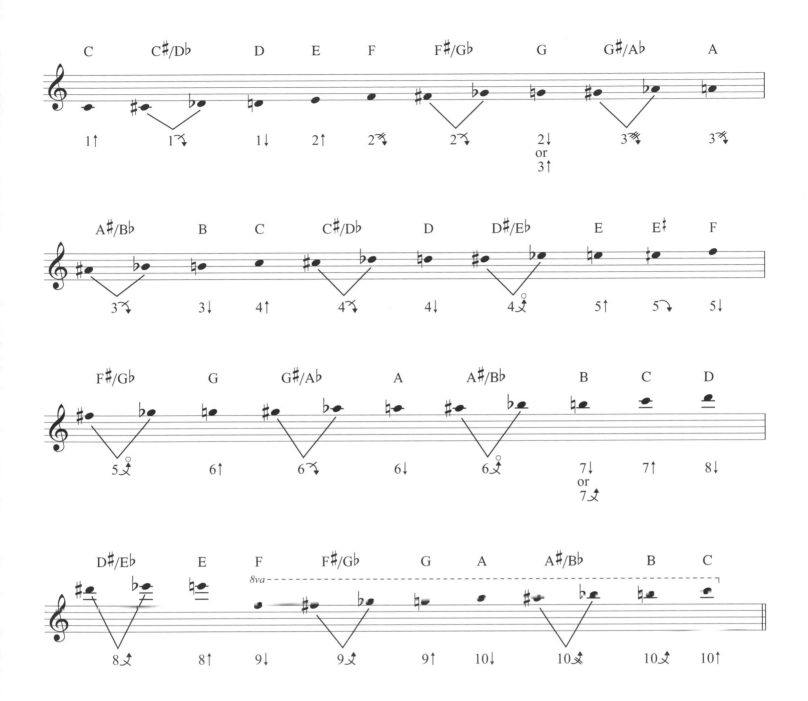

HARMONICA NOTATION LEGEND

Harmonica music can be notated two different ways: on a *musical staff*, and in *tablature*.

THE MUSICAL STAFF shows pitches and rhythms and is divided by bar lines into measures. Pitches are named after the first seven letters of the alphabet.

TABLATURE graphically represents the harmonica music. Each note will be accompanied by a number, 1 through 10, indicating what hole you are to play. The arrow that follows indicates whether to blow or draw. (All examples are shown using a C diatonic harmonica.)

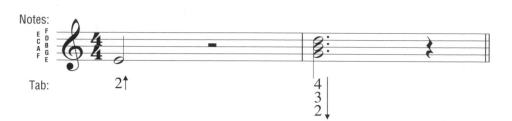

Blow (exhale) into 2nd hole.

Draw (inhale) 2nd, 3rd, & 4th holes together.

Notes on the C Harmonica

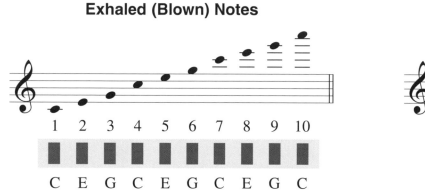

Exhaled (Blown) Notes

1 2 3 4 5 6 7 8 9 10

C E G C E G C E G C

Inhaled (Drawn) Notes

1 2 3 4 5 6 7 8 9 10

D G B D F A B D F A

Bends

Blow Bends

- 1/4 step
- 1/2 step
- 1 step
- 1 1/2 steps

Draw Bends

- 1/4 step
- 1/2 step
- 1 step
- 1 1/2 steps

Definitions for Special Harmonica Notation

SLURRED BEND: Play (draw) 3rd hole, then bend the note down one whole step.

GRACE NOTE BEND: Starting with a pre-bent note, immediately release bend to the target note.

VIBRATO: Begin adding vibrato to the sustained note on beat 3.

TONGUE BLOCKING: Using your tongue to block holes 2 & 3, play octaves on holes 1 & 4.

TRILL: Shake the harmonica rapidly to alternate between notes.

NOTE: Tablature numbers in parentheses are used when:

- The note is sustained, but a new articulation begins (such as vibrato), or
- The quantity of notes being sustained changes, or
- A change in dynamics (volume) occurs.
- It's the alternate note in a trill.

Additional Musical Definitions

D.S. al Coda
- Go back to the sign (𝄋), then play until the measure marked "***To Coda***," then skip to the section labelled "**Coda**."

D.C. al Fine
- Go back to the beginning of the song and play until the measure marked "***Fine***" (end).

- Repeat measures between signs.

 *(accent)*
- Accentuate the note (play initial attack louder).

(staccato)
- Play the note short.

1. 2.
- When a repeated section has different endings, play the first ending only the first time and the second ending only the second time.

Dynamics

p
- Piano (soft)

mp
- Mezzo Piano (medium soft)

mf
- Mezzo Forte (medium loud)

f
- Forte (loud)

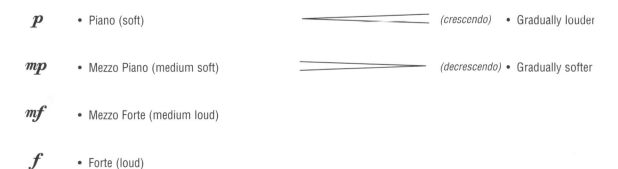 *(crescendo)*
- Gradually louder

(decrescendo)
- Gradually softer

HAL·LEONARD® HARMONICA PLAY-ALONG

Play your favorite songs quickly and easily!

Just follow the notation, listen to the audio to hear how the harmonica should sound, and then play along using the separate full-band backing tracks. The melody and lyrics are also included in the book in case you want to sing, or to simply help you follow along. The audio includes playback tools so you can adjust the recording to any tempo without changing pitch!

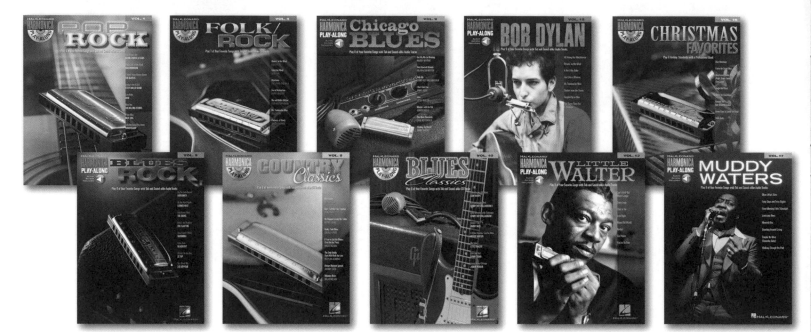

1. Pop/Rock
And When I Die • Bright Side of the Road • I Should Have Known Better • Low Rider • Miss You • Piano Man • Take the Long Way Home • You Don't Know How It Feels.
00000478 Book/CD Pack.........................$16.99

2. Rock Hits
Cowboy • Hand in My Pocket • Karma Chameleon • Middle of the Road • Run Around • Smokin' in the Boys Room • Train in Vain • What I like About You.
00000479 Book/CD Pack.........................$14.99

3. Blues/Rock
Big Ten Inch Record • On the Road Again • Roadhouse Blues • Rollin' and Tumblin' • Train Kept A-Rollin' • Train, Train • Waitin' for the Bus • You Shook Me.
00000481 Book/Online Audio $15.99

4. Folk/Rock
Blowin' in the Wind • Catch the Wind • Daydream • Eve of Destruction • Me and Bobby McGee • Mr. Tambourine Man • Pastures of Plenty.
00000482 Book/CD Pack.........................$14.99

5. Country Classics
Blue Bayou • Don't Tell Me Your Troubles • He Stopped Loving Her Today • Honky Tonk Blues • If You've Got the Money (I've Got the Time) • The Only Daddy That Will Walk the Line • Orange Blossom Special • Whiskey River.
00001004 Book/CD Pack.........................$14.99

6. Country Hits
Ain't Goin' down ('Til the Sun Comes Up) • Drive (For Daddy Gene) • Getcha Some • Here's a Quarter (Call Someone Who Cares) • Honkytonk U • One More Last Chance • Put Yourself in My Shoes • Turn It Loose.
00001013 Book/CD Pack $14.99

8. Pop Classics
Bluesette • Cherry Pink and Apple Blossom White • From Me to You • Love Me Do • Midnight Cowboy • Moon River • Peg O' My Heart • A Rainy Night in Georgia.
00001090 Book/Online Audio $14.99

9. Chicago Blues
Blues with a Feeling • Easy • Got My Mo Jo Working • Help Me • I Ain't Got You • Juke • Messin' with the Kid.
00001091 Book/Online Audio.................$15.99

10. Blues Classics
Baby, Scratch My Back • Eyesight to the Blind • Good Morning Little Schoolgirl • Honest I Do • I'm Your Hoochie Coochie Man • My Babe • Ride and Roll • Sweet Home Chicago.
00001093 Book/CD Pack $15.99

11. Christmas Carols
Angels We Have Heard on High • Away in a Manger • Deck the Hall • The First Noel • Go, Tell It on the Mountain • Jingle Bells • Joy to the World • O Little Town of Bethlehem.
00001296 Book/CD Pack...........................$12.99

12. Bob Dylan
All Along the Watchtower • Blowin' in the Wind • It Ain't Me Babe • Just like a Woman • Mr. Tambourine Man • Shelter from the Storm • Tangled up in Blue • The Times They Are A-Changin'.
00001326 Book/Online Audio.................$16.99

13. Little Walter
Can't Hold Out Much Longer • Crazy Legs • I Got to Go • Last Night • Mean Old World • Rocker • Sad Hours • You're So Fine.
00001334 Book/Online Audio $14.99

14. Jazz Standards
Autumn Leaves • Georgia on My Mind • Lullaby of Birdland • Meditation (Meditacao) • My Funny Valentine • Satin Doll • Some Day My Prince Will Come • What a Wonderful World.
00001335 Book/CD Pack..........................$16.99

15. Jazz Classics
All Blues • Au Privave • Comin' Home Baby • Song for My Father • Sugar • Sunny • Take Five • Work Song.
00001336 Book/CD Pack $14.99

16. Christmas Favorites
Blue Christmas • Frosty the Snow Man • Here Comes Santa Claus (Right down Santa Claus Lane) • Jingle-Bell Rock • Nuttin' for Christmas • Rudolph the Red-Nosed Reindeer • Santa Claus Is Comin' to Town • Silver Bells.
00001350 Book/CD Pack $14.99

17. Muddy Waters
Blow, Wind, Blow • Forty Days and Forty Nights • Good Morning Little Schoolgirl • Louisiana Blues • Mannish Boy • Standing Around Crying • Trouble No More (Someday Baby) • Walking Through the Park.
00821043 Book/Online Audio.................$14.99